I WANT TO BE . . . BOOK SERIES
Creator/Producer: Stephanie Maze, Maze Productions
Writer and Educational Consultant: Catherine O'Neill Grace
Designer: Lisa Lytton-Smith

Photographers for I WANT TO BE A VETERINARIAN:
Nicole Bengevino, Barbara Ries, Annie Griffiths Belt,
Gerd Ludwig, Steve Mellon, Karen Kasmauski,
Peter Menzel, Michael Nichols,
Joanna Pinneo, Joel Sartore

Other books in this series:
I WANT TO BE AN ASTRONAUT
I WANT TO BE A DANCER
I WANT TO BE AN ENGINEER
I WANT TO BE A CHEF

Copyright © 1997 by Maze Productions
Photography credits appear on page 48.

For information about permission to reproduce
selections from this book, please write to Permissions,
Houghton Mifflin Harcourt Publishing Company
215 Park Avenue South NY NY 10003.

Library of Congress Cataloging-in-Publication Data
Maze, Stephanie
I want to be a veterinarian/by Stephanie Maze and Catherine O'Neill Grace
p. cm. — (I want to be . . . book series)
Summary: Provides an overview of what is involved in
veterinary medicine and related fields.
ISBN 0-15-201296-6
1. Veterinarians—Juvenile literature. 2. Veterinary medicine—
Vocational guidance—Juvenile literature.
[1. Veterinarians. 2. Occupations.] I. Grace, Catherine O'Neill, 1950–
II. Title. III. Series.
SF756.M28 1997
636.089'06952—dc20 96-215

ISBN 0-15-201965-0 pb
SCP   16 17 18 19 20
4500529140

Pre-press through PrintNet
Printed and bound by RR Donnelley, China

I Want to Be...

A VETERINARIAN

Houghton Mifflin Harcourt
Boston   New York

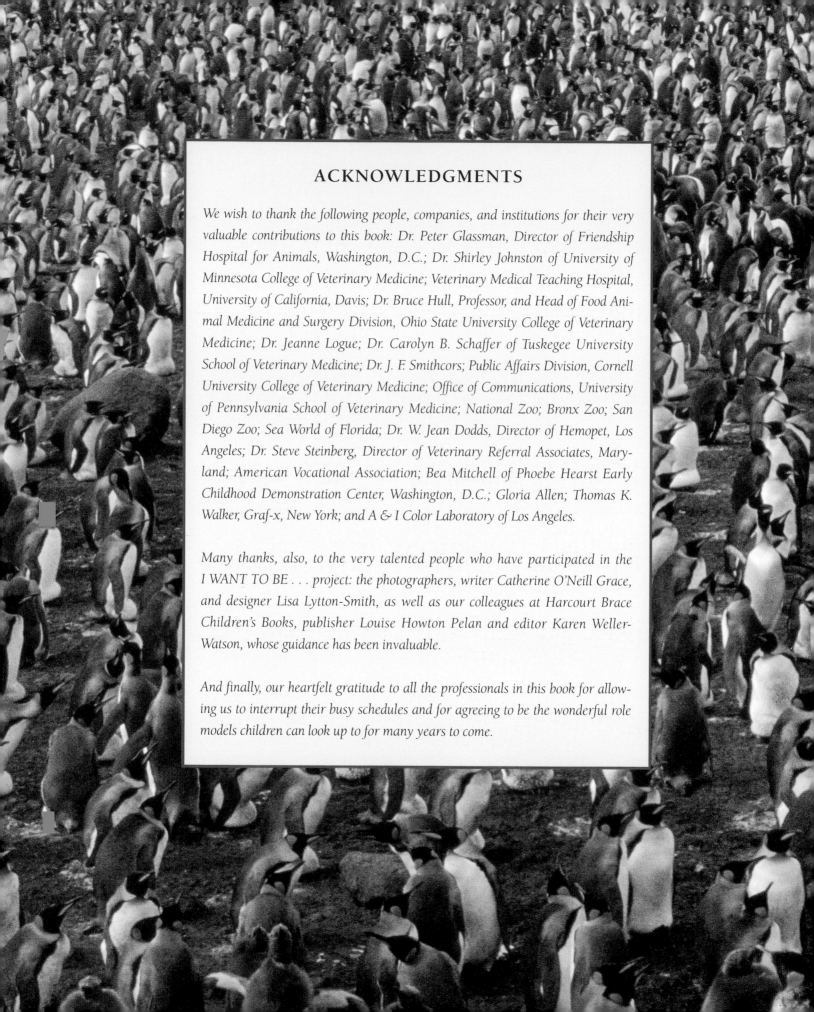

ACKNOWLEDGMENTS

We wish to thank the following people, companies, and institutions for their very valuable contributions to this book: Dr. Peter Glassman, Director of Friendship Hospital for Animals, Washington, D.C.; Dr. Shirley Johnston of University of Minnesota College of Veterinary Medicine; Veterinary Medical Teaching Hospital, University of California, Davis; Dr. Bruce Hull, Professor, and Head of Food Animal Medicine and Surgery Division, Ohio State University College of Veterinary Medicine; Dr. Jeanne Logue; Dr. Carolyn B. Schaffer of Tuskegee University School of Veterinary Medicine; Dr. J. F. Smithcors; Public Affairs Division, Cornell University College of Veterinary Medicine; Office of Communications, University of Pennsylvania School of Veterinary Medicine; National Zoo; Bronx Zoo; San Diego Zoo; Sea World of Florida; Dr. W. Jean Dodds, Director of Hemopet, Los Angeles; Dr. Steve Steinberg, Director of Veterinary Referral Associates, Maryland; American Vocational Association; Bea Mitchell of Phoebe Hearst Early Childhood Demonstration Center, Washington, D.C.; Gloria Allen; Thomas K. Walker, Graf-x, New York; and A & I Color Laboratory of Los Angeles.

Many thanks, also, to the very talented people who have participated in the I WANT TO BE . . . project: the photographers, writer Catherine O'Neill Grace, and designer Lisa Lytton-Smith, as well as our colleagues at Harcourt Brace Children's Books, publisher Louise Howton Pelan and editor Karen Weller-Watson, whose guidance has been invaluable.

And finally, our heartfelt gratitude to all the professionals in this book for allowing us to interrupt their busy schedules and for agreeing to be the wonderful role models children can look up to for many years to come.

To all children who dream the impossible dreams

Where to Start

If you love animals, you would probably love being a vet. That's what Dr. Candace Ashley, a veterinarian in Washington, D.C., always wanted to be. Dr. Ashley cares for small animals that people keep as companions—pets like cats, dogs, rabbits, and guinea pigs. At right, she's examining a kitten.

Dr. Ashley loves teaching families what they need to know to have happy, healthy pets. She says, "If I educate you to have a healthy dog, your child will learn in turn how to raise a healthy dog. It goes on generation after generation."

When Dr. Ashley is not working with animals and people, she is writing as "Dr. Kind" for a Humane Society newspaper. She answers questions young readers send in about their pets.

After college, Dr. Ashley spent four years at Tuskegee University's veterinary school in Alabama in the 1970s. Back then there weren't many women attending vet school. That has changed; today's classes are about 60 percent women.

If you would you like to prepare to be a doctor of veterinary medicine (D.V.M.) at one of the twenty-seven vet schools in the United States, Dr. Ashley says to study hard! She also suggests spending time working directly—or "hands-on"—with animals. Look for volunteer jobs or summer programs where you can work with a vet or in a kennel. Taking care of a pet of your own—whether it's a turtle, goldfish, cat, dog, or pony—will also teach you a lot about animals and their needs.

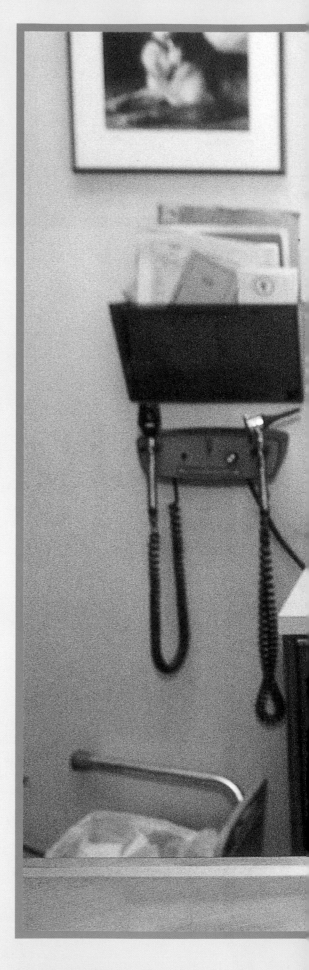

Vets at Work

Where do vets head when they leave for work in the morning?

That depends on what kind of vets they are. Many go to their offices or clinics to care for people's pets. Nearly half of the vets in the United States work with companion animals, doing everything from checkups to surgery to emergency care.

Did you know that some vets—like Dr. Flo Mitchell, of Washington, D.C., in small photo at near right—make house calls? She's treating a poodle named Lika for an ear infection. Lika's owner, Deborah Norton, offers comfort and helps hold the dog still.

But when your patient is a seven-gill shark, you might not want to treat it where it lives! At right, Dr. Tom Williams, a marine veterinarian at the Monterey Bay Aquarium in California, is taking a sample of tissue to try to diagnose what's causing a sore on the shark's nose. To prevent dehydration, his patient is safely enclosed in a small tank of water during the procedure.

Some vets choose to work in zoological parks. At far right, Dr. Amy Shima prepares material for a laboratory test at the San Diego Zoo. Dr. Shima also works directly with animals, doing things like examining lions or weighing newborn howler monkeys. Zoo vets work to keep the unusual animals in their care healthy. They also help wildlife biologists figure out how to keep threatened or endangered species alive in the wild.

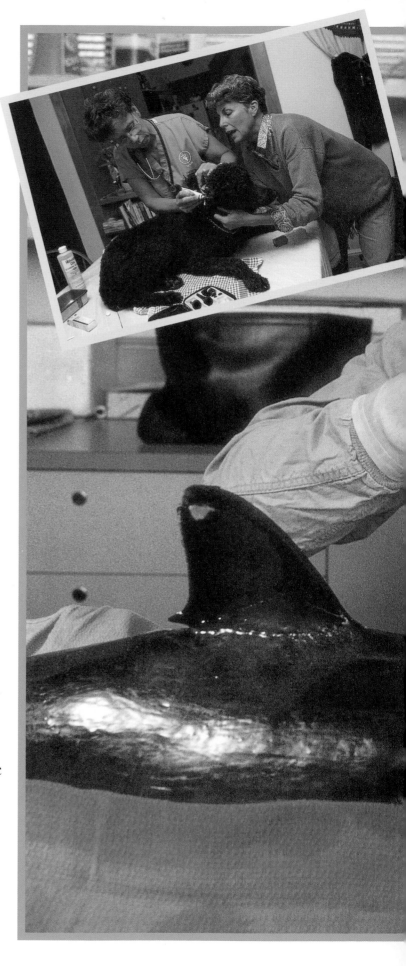

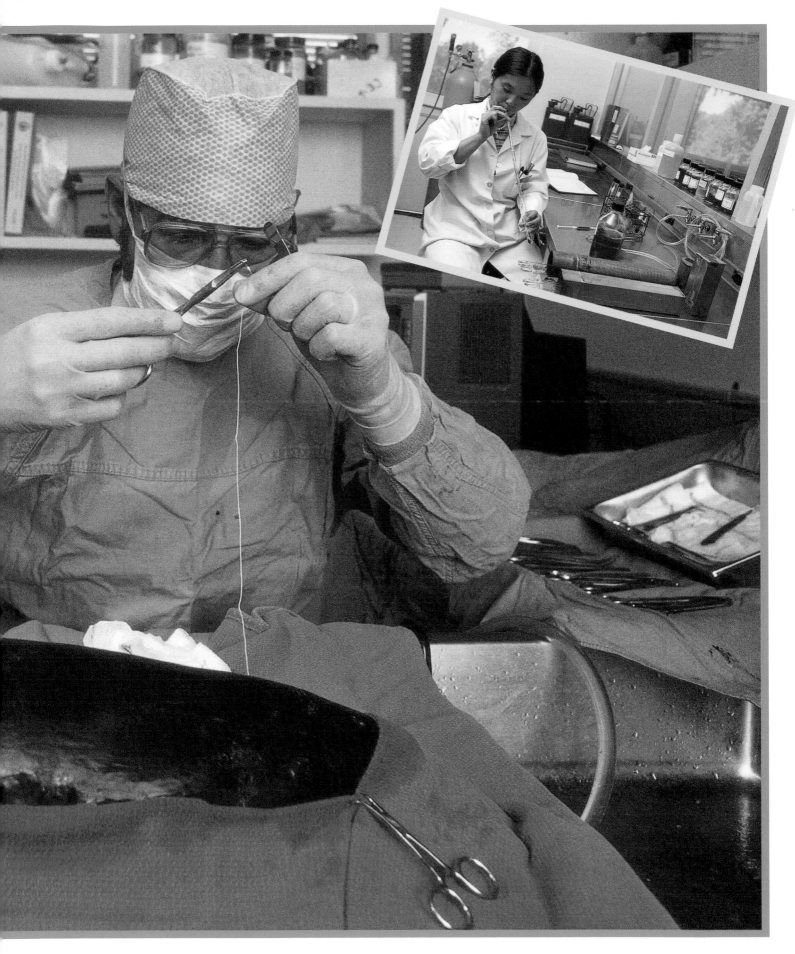

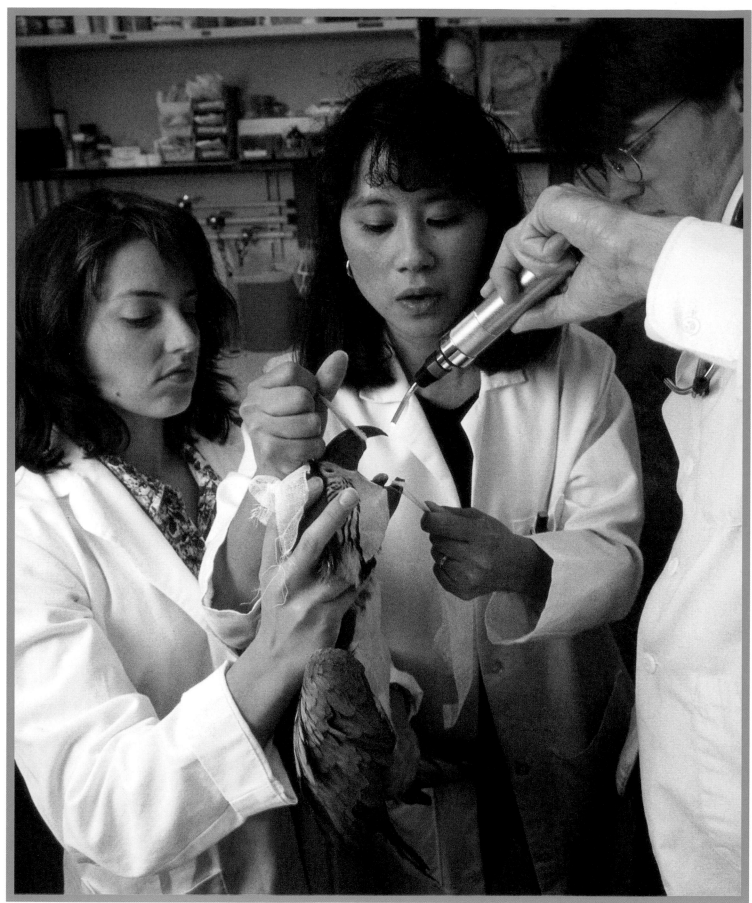

Exotic Animal Vet

Vets work with an amazing variety of animals. Exotic animal vets—such as Dr. Lisa Tell, center, in the photo at left—care for rare birds like this macaw, which is being treated at the University of California, Davis, Veterinary Medical Teaching Hospital. If you become an exotic animal vet, you might see monkeys, iguanas, ferrets, potbellied pigs, and all kinds of other animals in your day-to-day practice.

Large animal vets spend time caring for—you guessed it!—large animals. These include cows, sheep, and other farm animals—even llamas. At right, Dr. Bruce Hull, a professor at Ohio State University, helps a student check on a calf's heartbeat. Equine vets such as Dr. Rodrigo Vazquez de Mercado of the University of California, Davis, specialize in treating horses. Student Carrie Coit lends the vet a hand by holding a horse as he bandages its leg.

When people get sick, they can choose from many different therapies to help them feel better. Pet owners in Takoma Park, Maryland, can also choose unusual treatment for their animals. Dr. Monique Maniet runs her holistic veterinary practice there. Holistic medicine, whether for people or animals, looks at a patient's health and lifestyle as a whole, instead of treating each symptom separately.

Wesley, a five-year-old black Labrador, came to Dr. Maniet with severe skin allergies. "Wesley was treated with homeopathic medicine, nutrition, and acupuncture," Dr. Maniet says. "He has been improving steadily. His coat is better than ever!"

Whatever type of practice vets choose, they share these goals from the veterinarian's oath: to protect animal health and to relieve animal suffering.

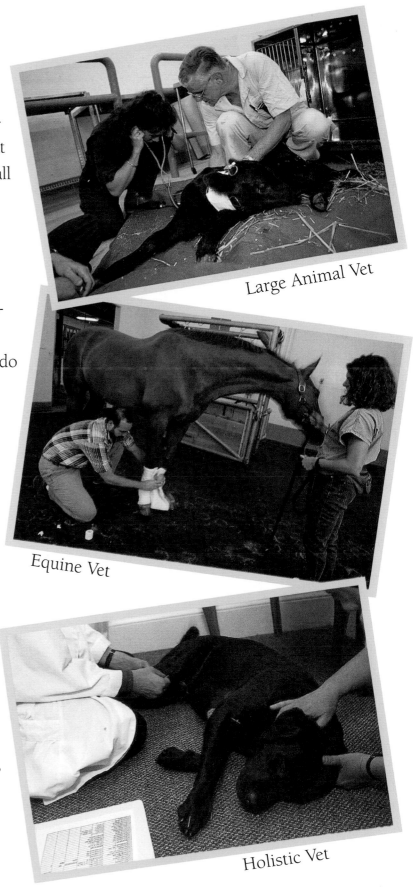

Large Animal Vet

Equine Vet

Holistic Vet

A Zoo Vet's Day

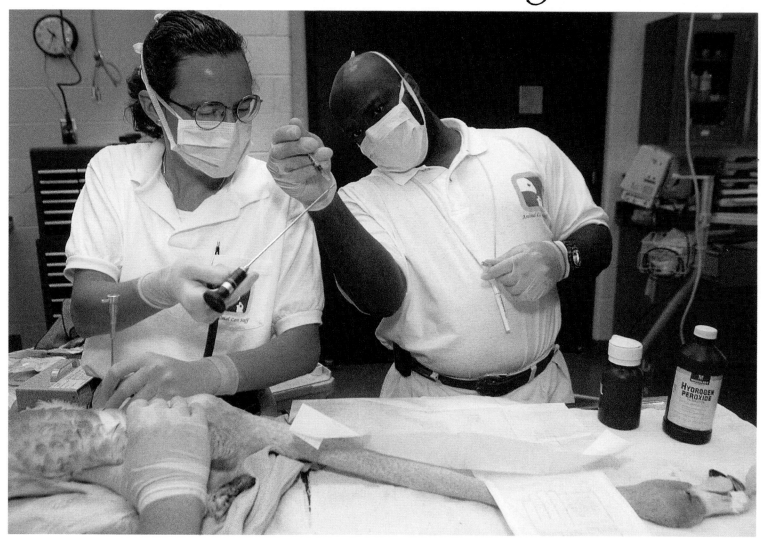

Here's your patient list so far today, Doctor: A flamingo. A rhinoceros iguana. A South American spectacled bear. There's an armadillo, too.

That unusual combination of animals is all in a day's work for Dr. Lucy Spelman, a veterinarian at the Smithsonian's National Zoological Park in Washington, D.C. The pictures on these pages show Dr. Spelman and her colleagues as they treat some of the animals at the zoo. Above, Dr. Spelman and Dr. Robert Davis perform surgery on a flamingo's wing.

A zoo vet's day includes routine care— like giving bears their physicals (left). It may also include emergency treatment of animals that have been injured. The armadillo at right hurt its carapace, or shell, and its tail. "He may have been trying to dig somewhere in his enclosure where the wall is rough," says Dr. Spelman. The armadillo's keeper alerted members of the vet staff, who then sprang into action.

"We give all the animals regular checkups," says Dr. Spelman. At right, keeper Monica Holland holds an iguana while Dr. Davis performs a routine physical examination.

It takes a big team to check up on a five-hundred-pound spectacled bear. In photo below right, Dr. Spelman and her colleagues roll Roger onto a table to give him an anesthetic, medicine to make him sleep so he feels no pain during the exam. With her, from left, are vet student Sonja Olson, hospital keeper Stephen Schultz, Dr. Davis, and head vet Dr. Richard Cambre.

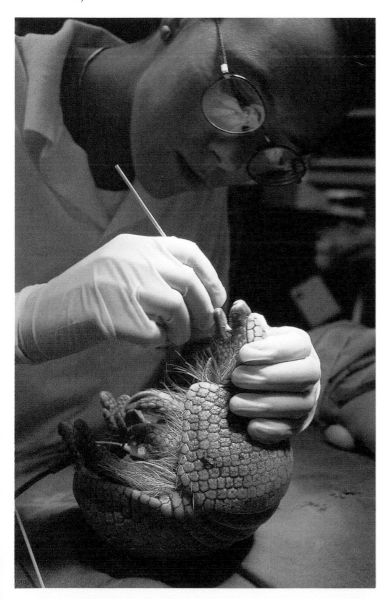

The bear's already asleep. Dr. Spelman administered the first dose of anesthetic with a dart gun while Roger was still in his enclosure. Then he was brought to the zoo hospital. The tube Dr. Spelman is holding will be used to give Roger gas that will keep him asleep as the doctors clean his teeth, trim his nails, and assess his general health.

"One of the greatest challenges in working with wild animals is getting them anesthetized and to the hospital safely," says Dr. Spelman. "Once they are under anesthesia and you can work on them, the procedures of surgery or maintenance health care are often much the same as a small animal vet might do on a dog."

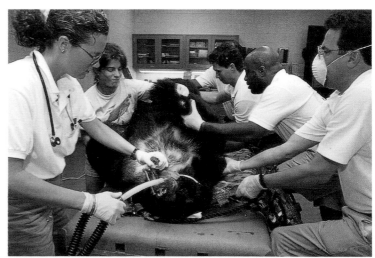

Specialist Vets

You've probably already encountered a lot of different doctors in your life. When you were born, an obstetrician or a midwife helped. Your baby and childhood doctor is called a pediatrician. If you have allergies, you may see an allergist. Has anyone you know ever broken a bone? A pediatrician probably sent your friend to an orthopedist. The list goes on and on.

Veterinary medicine also includes many specialties. When a vet specializes, he or she treats just one aspect of an animal's health—and does it very, very well. Other vets refer their patients to specialists when they have unusual problems or need a particular type of care.

What kinds of things do vet specialists do? Lots of things! At Cornell University's veterinary school, for example, there are specialists in cardiology (treating the heart), oncology (treating cancer), and dermatology (treating skin ailments), among others.

Look carefully at the pictures on these pages. Each one provides clues about what the vets' specialties are. Dr. Maya Yamagata, of Ohio State University, a veterinary ophthalmologist, checks an older dog's eyes for cataracts. At far right, nutritionist veterinarian Ellen Dierenfeld, who works at the Bronx Zoo in New York, measures ingredients for a healthy diet. Dr. Mike Knoeckel, a veterinary neurologist at one of the most specialized clinics in the country—Veterinary Referral Associates of Maryland—studies X rays of an animal's spine.

Which veterinary specialty appeals to you?

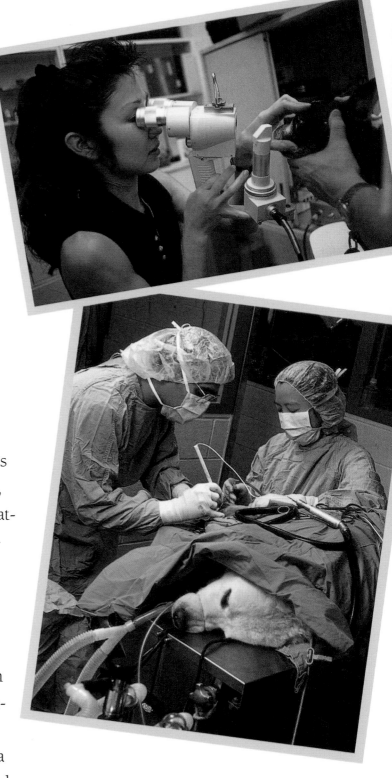

Orthopedic vets specialize in animals' skeletal structures—their bones, that is. At Angell Memorial Hospital near Boston, Dr. Paul Gambardella operates on a dog. Dr. Irene Takata assists.

Open wide. *Dr. Ronald Gammon, a vet dentist in Martinez, California, cleans a dog's teeth. The dog was anesthetized for the procedure. He won't bite!*

The History of Veterinary Science

What we call veterinary medicine has been around as long as human beings and animals have lived and worked together.

Historians have found Chinese writings about the diseases of horses, oxen, and buffalo that date back to 2,500 B.C. Indian art nearly four thousand years old shows men caring for horses and elephants. Ancient Egyptians' art shows their concern with the health of their cattle—and their dogs.

It's not surprising that cultures depending on animals for farming, food, and transportation developed ways to keep those animals healthy. Ancient Romans had a word for animal doctor. It's *veterinarius*. Does that sound familiar?

In about A.D. 500 a Roman wrote a book on the veterinary art. But for many centuries after Roman times, there wasn't much more recorded about the care of animals. A thousand years later another important book appeared. This one was called *Anatomy of the Horse*. It was written by an Italian, Carlo Ruini, in 1598, and is considered the first modern work in veterinary medicine.

For hundreds of years, people who worked with horses—called farriers—did much of the work vets would do today. Farriers were black-smiths who forged and applied iron shoes to horses' hooves to protect them. They also treated horses for injuries and illnesses. But they didn't go to college to learn their skills. They learned by working directly with animals. Farriers had

In the old days, men who treated animals didn't bother with white coats. "Cow doctor" William Carter dressed formally to administer medicine. His helper has his hands full keeping the patient quiet!

great practical skill, but they didn't know much about science. Some of the methods farriers used were primitive and painful—and didn't work.

The first scientific veterinary schools were established in Europe in the mid-eighteenth century—less than three hundred years ago. The field has grown fast since then. By the end of the nineteenth century, excellent veterinary schools had been established in the United States.

When Cornell University opened its doors in Ithaca, New York, in 1868, the vet school was just two rooms. Classes were taught by only one professor, Dr. James Law. Trained in Scotland, Dr. Law became the first professor of veterinary medicine in the United States.

James Law and Ezra Cornell, the founder of the university, shared a dream. They wanted to create a veterinary college that would educate doctors who were well trained in science as well as in practical skill with animals. Dr. Law was a famous teacher. But he was also a working vet. During his early years at the university, he was often called out to farms in the New York countryside around Cornell. He took his students along with him.

Dr. Law's dream came true in 1894 when the governor of New York signed an act establishing a state veterinary college at Cornell. In the century since then, Cornell has trained more than four thousand vets—including Dr. Martin J. Fettman, the first veterinarian astronaut.

Today there are more than two dozen schools of veterinary medicine in the United States. Their students master all sorts of ultramodern technology to practice their profession. But they still share something with the people who cared for livestock in ancient Egypt: They are devoted to keeping animals as healthy as possible.

The old-fashioned illustration above shows the University of Pennsylvania's vet school in 1887, three years after it opened. Students listened to lectures, made horseshoes, studied science and anatomy, treated exotic animals such as elephants, and attended to small companion animals, just as vets do today. The well-dressed lady at top left has brought her little dog to the vet school for treatment.

Left: Only one woman, seated in front in this photograph, graduated from the College of Veterinary Medicine at Cornell in 1910. Florence Kimball was the first woman in the United States to become a vet.

Vets Go High Tech

CT scans. Video. Kidney dialysis machines. Hip replacement operations. Heart bypasses. Laser surgery. Ultrasound machines.

It's not unusual to use high-tech equipment and procedures at modern hospitals. But some folks think it's a little odd for vets to use high-tech equipment and demanding surgical techniques on their patients—dogs, cats, horses, birds, reptiles . . .

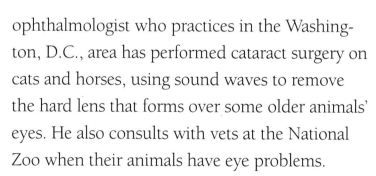

More and more vets, however, are taking advantage of advanced medical equipment and techniques to treat their patients. In many places veterinary medicine has gone high tech. For example, the operating room at the University of California, Davis, looks as complex and up-to-date as any operating room for people. That's because it is! In the photo above, hip surgery is being performed on a small animal. Vets at the university have also performed open-heart surgery on dogs and kidney transplants on cats.

California may be on the cutting edge of high-tech veterinary medicine, but doctors elsewhere are getting into the action, too.

For instance, Dr. Seth Koch, a veterinary ophthalmologist who practices in the Washington, D.C., area has performed cataract surgery on cats and horses, using sound waves to remove the hard lens that forms over some older animals' eyes. He also consults with vets at the National Zoo when their animals have eye problems.

Are these modern techniques expensive? You bet! That's why some pet owners have started to buy medical insurance for their companion animals in case the day arrives when their pet needs a computerized tomography (CT) scan or a heart bypass operation. A typical policy costs $134 a year. But a hip-joint replacement would cost $1,500—more than ten times as much.

A closer look. *At the University of California, Davis, vets use CT scanning technology to examine a horse's brain for abnormalities. The technology gives doctors a unique view into an animal. It creates thin cross-sectional images of the body without making a single incision. The images appear on a computer screen.*

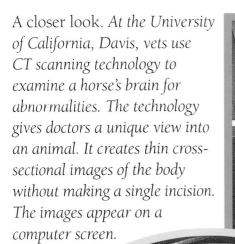

Left, Dr. Brett Sponseiler monitors the movable equipment on a CT machine as a horse is moved inside. Meanwhile, at the computer screen, technician Paul Mickel and student Betty Theriault program the scanner to select specific areas of the horse's head for viewing.

Video for iguanas. *At the San Diego Zoo, right, a researcher shows a captive male iguana videotaped images of another male iguana. The experiment is designed to show how the reptiles respond to other males in the species. With only one iguana around, the researcher uses technology to stimulate a response.*

Did You Know . . .

. . . that people go to great heights to help save vanishing species? At right, field biologist and conservationist Eduardo Nycander von Massenbach hangs one hundred feet up in the Peruvian rainforest as he checks a young macaw for parasites. He will return the chick to its nest after he weighs and measures it.

. . . that veterinarians in the United States care for some 55 million cats, 52 million dogs, 11.7 million birds, and more than 7 million other companion animals?

. . . that the ancient Greeks called veterinarians *hippiatroi*, which means "horse doctors"?

. . . that during the Middle Ages in Europe, many people believed that sick animals were possessed by evil spirits? Superstitions developed, such as the idea that nailing horseshoes above a barn door could keep demons away from the animals inside. Some people still consider horseshoes lucky.

. . . that the two most popular canine breeds registered with the American Kennel Club are Labrador retrievers and German shepherd dogs?

. . . that dogs with crooked teeth can be fitted with braces?

. . . that research veterinarians are actively involved in the effort to find medicines to fight AIDS and other diseases humans get?

. . . that vets can choose among twenty different board-certified specialties? To qualify, vets must complete a residency of up to five years in their specialty and pass an exam—and that's *after* they finish vet school!

. . . that most veterinarians work fifty or more hours per week?

. . . that the American humorist Will Rogers admired vets? He said, "Personally, I have always felt that the best doctor is the veterinarian. He can't ask his patient what is the matter. He's just got to know."

Hands-on Learning

Michelle Freese enjoys grooming her Dorset sheep to perfection before entering her in the Ohio State Fair in Columbus (left).

Before you commit yourself to working in the field of veterinary medicine, it's a good idea to get up close and personal with animals to see how you like it, the way the kids on these pages are doing.

In the summer you could go to camp or seek out work experiences that bring you and animals together. Whenever you travel, include animals on the itinerary. The lucky kids in the photo above right are getting to know a bottle-nosed dolphin in an education program at the Dolphin Quest Learning Center in Hawaii.

At right, a 4-H Club member scrubs his pig in preparation for the Montgomery County Fair in Maryland. If these teenagers decide to work as large animal vets, they'll already be familiar with their patients when the time comes.

There are lots of other possibilities! You can work in a 4-H Club, help out with animals on a farm, or volunteer at a zoo or animal clinic that needs extra hands. Or your class could invite an animal specialist to visit your school. That's what some first graders in Palo Cedro, California, did. But Ryan Stephani, the boy in the large photo at far right, wasn't too sure he wanted to get close to the llama that veterinar-

ian Dr. Betsy Anderson brought to the class. Here's one more good idea: Ask your parents to let you take responsibility for the care of your pet, including going along to the vet for checkups.

Left, in New York, as part of the Bronx Zoo's Teen Internship Program, two students write down observations about turtles. The Bronx Zoo established the world's first zoo-education department in 1929.

Getting to know you. *In Lincoln, Massachusetts, a participant in City Bound, a program that takes urban kids to the country, feeds a goat (left). For many youngsters, the program is their first experience with farm animals.*

Horse Camp

Is spending a week in the Virginia countryside, thinking about nothing but horses, your idea of heaven? Then you'd love Camp 3H. That stands for Hippology, Horse Bowl, and Horse Judging.

Hippology has nothing to do with hips. It's a field of study that involves knowing all the characteristics of different breeds so that you can judge horses. The second *H*—Horse Bowl— is a fun, competitive quiz show about horses that campers participate in. Horse Judging, the third *H*, stands for the opportunity kids at the camp get to try judging a horse show themselves.

Camp 3H *isn't* about riding. "This camp really concentrates on how to accurately judge the quality of a horse. . . . We teach the structural correctness of each breed," says Fae Herbert, director of the camp. "Horses are built very differently. Some are well suited for jumping, some for trail riding, some for hunting, some for racing."

Kids ages nine to thirteen who are members of the 4-H Club can attend Camp 3H. Part of the camp experience involves learning about horse physiology and horse illnesses from a visiting equine vet.

"The goal of Camp 3H is for the kids to become better horse people," says the director. That's what campers Jennifer Durbin and Mary Truban are working on at left. They're busy recording their observations of Arabian mares.

Of course, camp is not *all* business. In the small photo at far left, Stacy Lambert pauses to make friends with Rainbow, a horse who lives at Georgetown Farm in Free Union, Virginia.

Later on, Stacy (in background of photo below) watches with friends while Jesse James, another horse at Georgetown Farm, undergoes an examination. Dr. Louis Johnson, an equine vet, demonstrates how to examine a horse's eye. Another camper, Amy McDaniel, uses a stethoscope to listen to Jesse James's heart in photo at top right. In the middle photo, Karla Priddy notes her opinion of hunter Lad's stride, pace, and obedience to his rider.

Do any of the campers want to be large animal veterinarians? Absolutely! Then they would get to spend all their time with horses—not just a week!

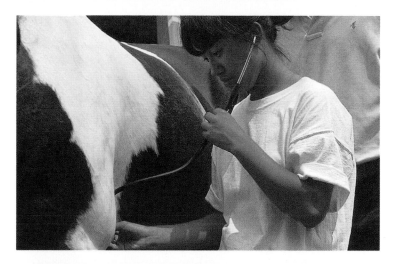

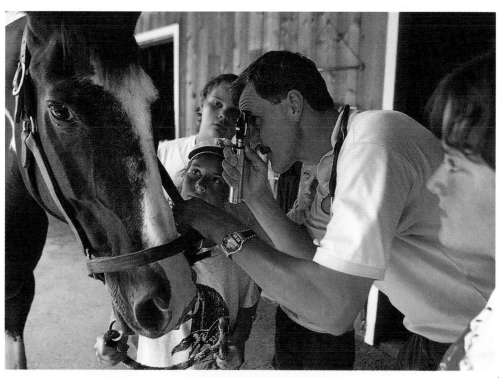

Vets and Vet Techs in Training

The future vets you've met so far are young enough to dream—without having to make any big decisions yet. On these two pages, you'll get acquainted with some high school and college age students who are very serious about careers in veterinary medicine. They're *almost* ready to go out and get real jobs.

Some of these students have decided to train for positions in the technical side of animal health care. They won't be attending four years of vet school, but they will be learning skills for a career caring for animals. They will become nurses, surgical assistants, anesthesia assistants, and more.

The two photographs at lower right capture the action in the surgery area used by students in a two-year veterinary technology program at Northern Virginia Community College (NOVA). At right, student Barbara Menella monitors an anesthetized cat before surgery. Program director Dr. Leslie Sinn checks to make sure everything is OK. After the surgery, one tech student bandages the cat's leg after removing an intravenous needle. Another technician gently holds the animal.

Veterinary technicians are very important people! Their assistance frees vets to spend more time working with clients and patients. Often, techs are the professionals who comfort and care for sick animals before and after

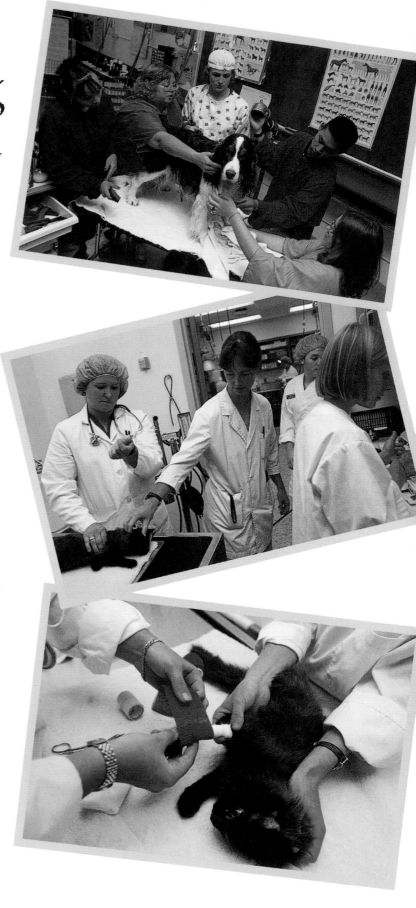

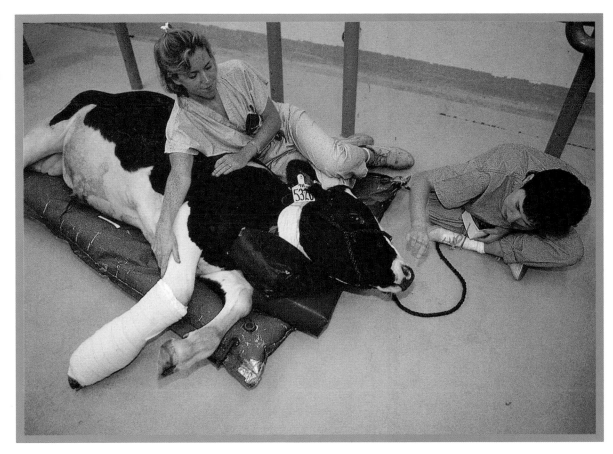

Real-life experience. *In all these pictures, students learn by doing. At far left, under the watchful eyes of instructor Janet Kolakoski (in cap), Ebony Rubeck, Elizabeth Woodard, Wendy Hawes, and Binh Nguyen—high school seniors at the Chantilly Professional Technical Center in Virginia— carefully brush and blow-dry Clue, an English springer spaniel. As they train, the students also operate a grooming business for the community.*

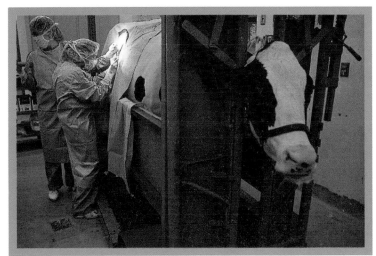

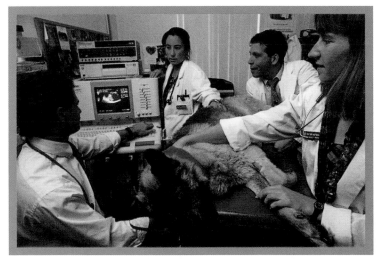

medical procedures. They need to be patient, compassionate people.

In large photo at top of page, Brigid Lenahan and fellow student Nora Collins comfort a bull calf recovering from surgery on an infected joint. Above left, Tina Wilson and Teresa Costa treat a cow with an abdominal tumor. All these students attend Ohio State University.

Even a high-tech procedure like performing ultrasound on a dog's heart calls for students' healing hands (above right). As Dr. Richard Kienle of the University of California, Davis, runs the test, students Lisa Shimomura, Brian Baumgard, and Heather Hartwick pat the patient.

Vets and vet techs in training will tell you that their education gives new meaning to *hands-on*.

Veterinarian Vocabulary

Like any profession, veterinary medicine comes with tools of the trade. Here are some things that vets and their assistants use as they examine animals, diagnose their illnesses, and perform surgery to cure them. Some of these pieces of equipment are found only in high-tech centers; others can be slipped into a doctor's pocket or medical bag and carried along on a call.

SURGICAL TOOLS

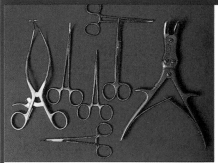

Various surgical instruments are laid out on a table ready for use. Some of these clamps might be used to hold sutures (thread) as a surgeon sews incisions up after surgery. The biggest tool, at right, is called a rongeur. It's used to fix bones during orthopedic operations. Before these tools are used, they are carefully sterilized to kill germs.

STETHOSCOPE

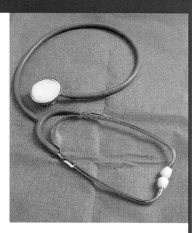

A stethoscope is one of the most basic—and one of the most important—tools of a vet's trade. It amplifies heart and lung sounds, making them loud enough so that the doctor can hear them clearly. Many doctors, for humans and for animals, keep their stethoscopes in a pocket or around their necks at all times.

X RAYS

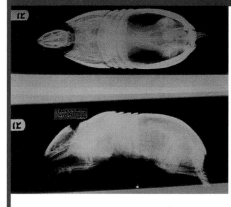

With carefully controlled doses of X rays, veterinarians can take pictures of bones without performing surgery. X rays were discovered in 1895 by W. C. Roentgen. Their use has made diagnosing many problems much easier—for patients as well as doctors!

SURGICAL MASK

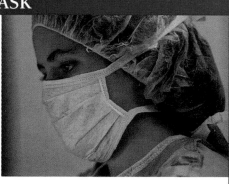

A veterinary student, scrubbed—or washed so that she's germfree—and ready for surgery at Ohio State University, wears a surgical mask, cap, and gown made of materials designed to reduce the patient's exposure to germs during a medical procedure.

INTRAVENOUS CATHETER

During surgery or while a patient is recovering, medicines or fluids can be put into the body through this tube, which goes into a vein. Did you notice that the person inserting a syringe into the catheter is wearing surgical gloves to prevent the spread of infection?

INDIRECT OPHTHALMOSCOPE

This vet is using an instrument called an ophthalmoscope, which allows her to check for damage to the retina, or back part, of her patient's eye. The retina is the part of the eye that forms images. If it is damaged, an animal's vision is reduced or destroyed.

HOOF NIPPER

This object may look like pruning shears to use in the garden—but it's a veterinary tool. It's used to trim cows' tough hooves. Hooves, like human fingernails, are made of dead cells of a material called keratin. Animals have no feeling in their hooves, so this nipper won't hurt.

WHOLE BLOOD

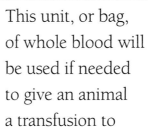

This unit, or bag, of whole blood will be used if needed to give an animal a transfusion to replace blood lost during surgery or after an accident. Transfusions can only be given within a species. That means dogs can only receive dog blood, cats can only receive cat blood, and so on.

ENDOTRACHEAL TUBES

One of these tubes is inserted into an animal's windpipe (trachea) to keep it open during surgery. The tube helps the animal breathe while it's asleep during anesthesia. The tubes come in a variety of sizes to fit the tracheas of different-size animals.

ELECTROCARDIOGRAPH MACHINE

When an animal's (or human's) heart beats, it gives off an electrical impulse, or signal. This machine monitors and measures the signals and charts them on a graph. Vets hook animals up to the machines to identify heart problems.

Helping Hands

What if you're thinking, *Vet school, giving anesthesia, performing surgery . . . That's not for me*, but you still want to work with animals?

Don't worry. There are lots of jobs to do. You could feed a giraffe, like this keeper putting acacia branches within neck-stretching reach at the San Diego Zoo. You could train a performing pseud-orca whale, as Liz Morris does at Sea World in Orlando, Florida. Or, like Randy Hamilton, assistant curator of husbandry operations at the Monterey Bay Aquarium in California, you could serve dinner to a giant octopus (far right). Randy says that giant octopuses enjoy being petted by the staff.

Is baby care more in your line? You could follow Pete Escobar's lead. He works in a chimp colony at the Southwest Foundation in Texas, where about 240 of the primates live. Here Pete cuddles and feeds a baby chimp as another one naps in an incubator nearby. Primate child care might also include blow-drying an orangutan's hair, as a keeper at the San Diego Zoo does for Karen after her bath (above).

Animal grooming takes up a lot of head elephant trainer Marie Galloway's time at the National Zoological Park in Washington, D.C. (top, far right). Toni, a twenty-nine-year-old female Asian elephant, needs a daily bath to keep her skin clean and healthy.

A Day at Friendship Animal Hospital

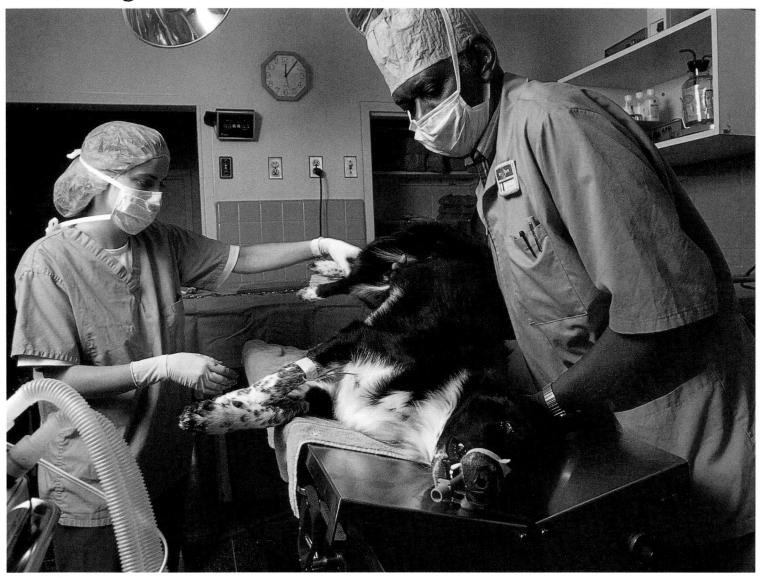

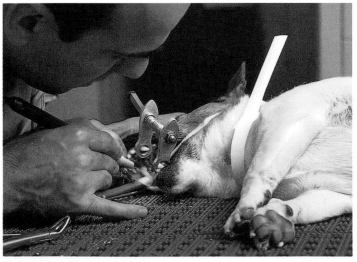

Welcome to Friendship Animal Hospital, a companion animal practice in Washington, D.C. Many families rely on the vets and support staff here to care for their beloved animals. Dozens of dogs, cats, and other pets visit the office every week.

As these photographs show, every day at Friendship is a busy one! Animals come in for routine checkups, for teeth cleanings, for grooming, and for more serious surgery. Friendship also provides emergency care twenty-four hours a day.

Vets who are closed in the evening often refer their emergency night calls to the vets at Friendship.

The vets, technicians, and other staff at Friendship know their animal patients by name. That's Alice, in the small photo at far left. She is having tartar removed from her teeth with an ultrasonic scanner. Veterinary technician Tanvir Avani does the procedure as Alice sleeps soundly under an anesthetic. An endotracheal tube in the dog's mouth and throat helps her breathe oxygen.

Left, veterinary surgical technician Tim Miller lifts Watkins from the surgery table after an operation. That's Dr. Marcie Duffey in the background. Watkins is going to be fine.

At right, Adrienne Collins, a Friendship staffer, trims Fluffy, a Persian cat. Below, ninth grader Tanner Scholz hugs her dog, Charlie, who's waiting to have his teeth cleaned. In the background, technician Tim Miller prepares another dog for surgery. It's just a normal day at Friendship Animal Hospital.

They couldn't do it without you! *At Friendship Animal Hospital, like any busy veterinary clinic, the support staff—including groomer Adrienne Collins and technicians Tim Miller and Tanvir Avani—help the practice thrive. Without them, routine care would be delayed while vets attended to surgery and emergency cases. Fluffy, the Persian cat above, might have preferred it that way. But Tanner Scholz and her dog, Charlie, at left, will be glad when Charlie's teeth are clean and he's back home again.*

In the Field: North America

Most veterinarians—almost 80 percent, according to the American Veterinary Medical Association—work in private practice. Nearly half of those vets work with small companion animals. Their patients are usually friendly—even cuddly.

Wildlife veterinarians and biologists, on the other hand, work with animals that you might not want to pet—like the crocodile that wildlife biologist Joe Wasilewski is measuring (right).

Work in the wild can be exciting. You are outdoors a lot of time, often in the wilderness. Your patients can be hard to locate, and even harder to catch for examination.

Veterinarian Mark Barone (above), who works for the New Opportunities in Animal Health Sciences (NOAHS) program based at the National Zoo in Washington, D.C., examines a sample from a Florida panther. His assistant holds the animal in the background. Barone is working in Florida's Big Cypress National Preserve. This kind of panther is one of the few large predators that have managed to survive in North America.

For adventurous people who love nature, love animals, and want to see threatened and endangered species survive on our planet, work in the wild is the way to go.

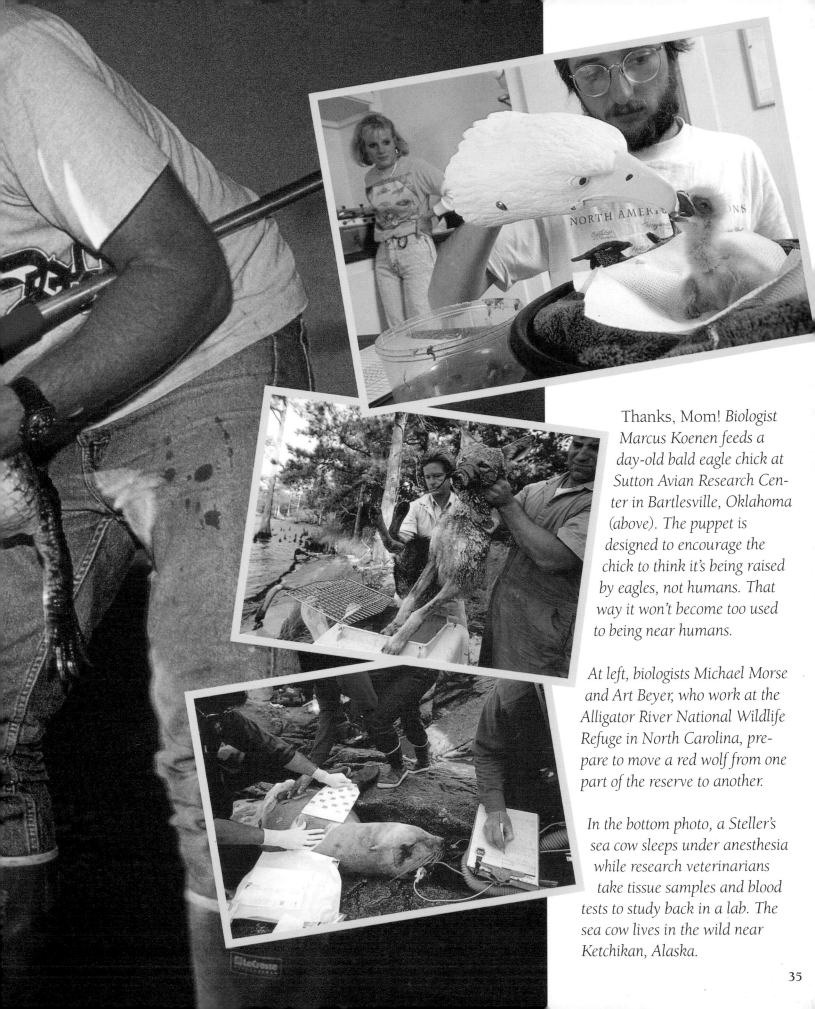

Thanks, Mom! *Biologist Marcus Koenen feeds a day-old bald eagle chick at Sutton Avian Research Center in Bartlesville, Oklahoma (above). The puppet is designed to encourage the chick to think it's being raised by eagles, not humans. That way it won't become too used to being near humans.*

At left, biologists Michael Morse and Art Beyer, who work at the Alligator River National Wildlife Refuge in North Carolina, prepare to move a red wolf from one part of the reserve to another.

In the bottom photo, a Steller's sea cow sleeps under anesthesia while research veterinarians take tissue samples and blood tests to study back in a lab. The sea cow lives in the wild near Ketchikan, Alaska.

In the Wild, around the World

Can you imagine yourself weighing gray-headed albatross chicks in Antarctica? Conducting blood tests on koala bears in Australia? Feeding macaws in the rainforest of Peru?

Those activities are all in a day's work for the conservation researchers on these pages. It's what the scientists love to do, and it's important to everyone on our planet.

Field biologist Eduardo Nycander von Massenbach was a successful architect in Lima, Peru, before he got involved in studying and saving macaws. Now he's the director of the Wildlife Conservation Society's macaw project.

Veterinarian Dr. Wendy Blanshard studies koalas at Lone Pine Koala Sanctuary near Brisbane, Australia. Although almost as much of a symbol of that country as the kangaroo, koalas struggle for survival. Their special habitat, eucalyptus forests, are shrinking as Australia develops. Research vets like Dr. Blanshard are working hard to keep Australia's remaining koalas healthy and to fight the changes that threaten the marsupials.

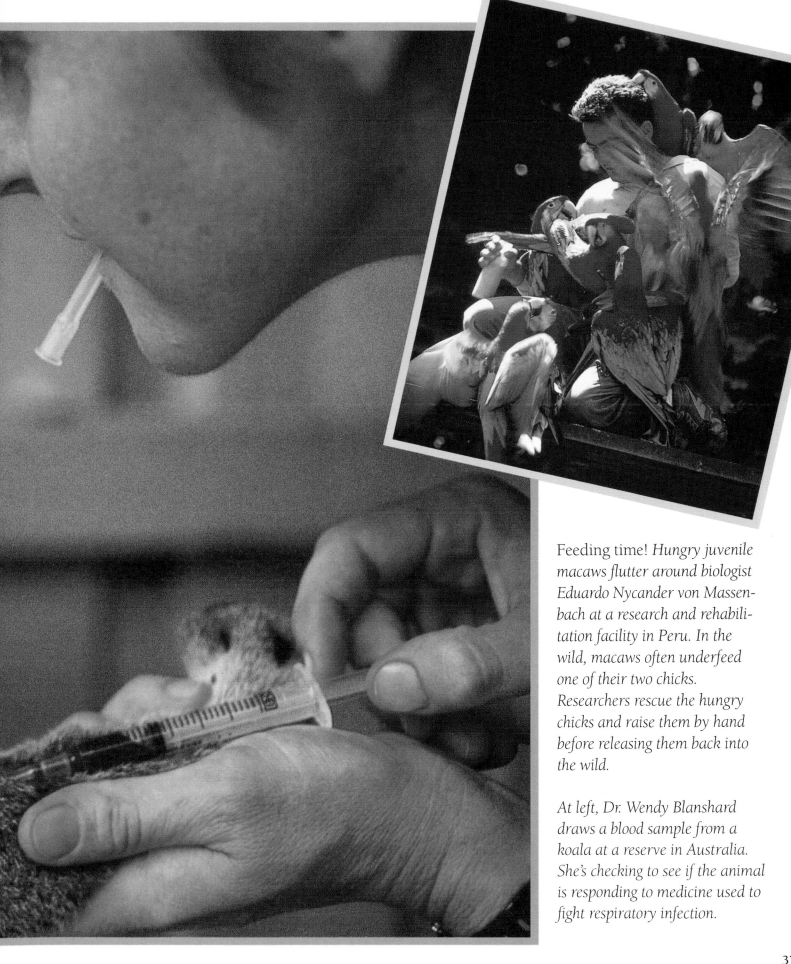

Feeding time! *Hungry juvenile macaws flutter around biologist Eduardo Nycander von Massenbach at a research and rehabilitation facility in Peru. In the wild, macaws often underfeed one of their two chicks. Researchers rescue the hungry chicks and raise them by hand before releasing them back into the wild.*

At left, Dr. Wendy Blanshard draws a blood sample from a koala at a reserve in Australia. She's checking to see if the animal is responding to medicine used to fight respiratory infection.

It takes stamina and patience to work with animals in the wild. Some researchers devote their lifetime to research, as Dr. Jane Goodall has done with the chimpanzees of Gombe National Park, in Tanzania. Dr. Goodall, a primatologist, began her work with chimps in 1960 and has made many important discoveries about them.

In China, Beijing University zoologist Pan Wenshi works hard to study and protect the giant panda. Over the years he has trained a new generation of scientists to continue his studies. He has also made the Chinese people more aware of the wonderful animals that hide in their forests.

All over the globe many dedicated animal scientists are struggling to study and save animals. If you were one of them, where in the world would you like to work?

Save the animals! *In China, zoologists Pan Wenshi and Lu Zhi examine a baby giant panda (left).*

In Tanzania, Dr. Jane Goodall observes the animals she knows so well: chimpanzees. Here, she watches as Pax, an orphaned chimp, raises his arm in a gesture that means "Groom me!" His brother Prof starts to respond. Dr. Goodall has learned a great deal about chimp communication and family structure in her thirty-five years of work in Gombe.

At left, researchers in Madagascar examine an anesthetized sifaka. Madagascar is home to many animals, including lemurs, that are found nowhere else on earth. But destruction of their habitats has driven many of the island nation's animals close to extinction.

An Old-Fashioned Practice

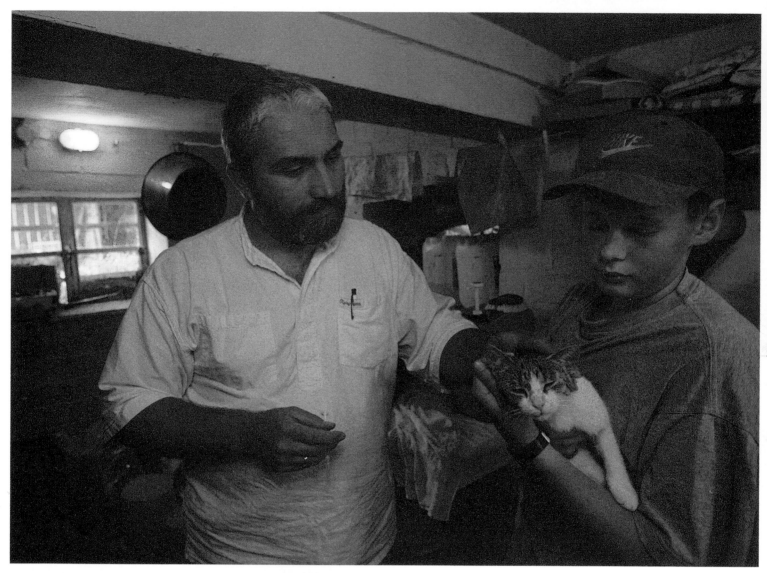

Cats and cows. Horses and dogs. Sheep, geese, chickens, and pigs. Long rides in the country. Midnight calls in all weather . . .

Dr. Uwe Scharf, who works in the country-side around Schwalmstadt, a small village in Germany, practices veterinary medicine the way it was done in the old days.

Dr. Scharf's patients don't come to him. He goes to them, driving his trusty Volvo station wagon with its tray of medicines, herbal remedies, and equipment loaded in the trunk (left).

He works early in the morning, at suppertime, in the middle of the night—whenever his patients need him.

Dr. Scharf's main responsibility is keeping the area's farm animals healthy. But he also treats small pets that live on the farms, like Mietzi, the cat in the photograph at left. Dr. Scharf is going to spay Mietzi so she won't have any more kittens. Her owner, Christoph Gutheil, cradles her before the surgery.

Raised next door to a farm, Dr. Scharf used to spend his spare time visiting the animals there. He thinks that experience influenced his decision to become a vet. He considers himself a defender of animals. He also loves to be outdoors and to travel around the countryside.

Being a rural vet has its disadvantages, however. Dr. Scharf can't make many plans in advance since he never knows when his patients

will need him. Being on call means that he can't always spend the time he'd like to with his family. Sometimes he wonders about working with other vets in a clinic instead of being on the road so much.

But then he decides it's worth it—especially when his patients get better, and become his friends.

A busy day. *In the photograph above, Dr. Uwe Scharf listens to the lungs of a horse that has caught a cold. He will treat the horse with a mixture of herbs added to its food.*

At left, Dr. Scharf examines a cow's infected hoof, which has a stone caught in it. The farmer's young daughters—Kathrin, Stefanie, and Christiana— watch the vet work. Dr. Scharf will remove the stone and bandage the cow's sore foot.

Some Famous Veterinarians

Many vets work hard throughout their careers, and the only people who recognize them are their clients—and the animals they helped, of course! Other vets have become household names. Read below about some of these famous veterinarians. Maybe your name will be added to this list someday!

DR. DANIEL E. SALMON
Dr. Salmon was the first chief of the Federal Bureau of Animal Industry, created by Congress in 1884 to battle animal diseases, and the first person in U.S. history to receive a D.V.M. (from Cornell). He discovered *Salmonella,* a disease-causing germ now named after him.

DR. COOPER CURTICE
Although many of his colleagues laughed at him, in 1890 Dr. Curtice suggested that ticks were spreading Texas fever, which was killing cattle all over the country. Curtice was right—and the epidemic was soon stopped!

DR. NATHANIEL LUSHINGTON
Dr. Lushington was born in 1869. He earned his degree from the University of Pennsylvania in 1897, becoming the first African American veterinary school graduate in the world.

DR. JAMES HERRIOT
Author of the best-seller *All Creatures Great and Small* and many other heartwarming and informative books about being a country animal doctor in England, Dr. Herriot continued to work as a rural vet until his death in 1995.

DR. ALFREDA J. WEBB
Dr. Webb was the first African American woman to graduate from a U.S. school of veterinary medicine. She graduated from Tuskegee University in Alabama in 1949. Dr. Webb practiced and taught veterinary medicine in Alabama and North Carolina for forty years. She died in 1994.

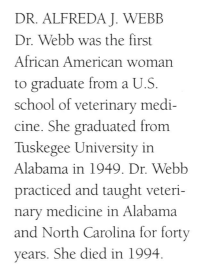

DR. W. JEAN DODDS

Dr. Dodds, a specialist in animal blood diseases, is the founder of Hemopet, the first nonprofit national blood bank program for animals, based in Irvine, California. She is shown here with Patches, a blood-donor greyhound.

DR. MARTIN J. FETTMAN

Dr. Fettman was the first veterinarian in space. An astronaut, he served on the space shuttle *Columbia* during its Life Sciences–2 mission in 1993. He ran gravity experiments using laboratory rats.

DR. SHIRLEY JOHNSTON

A leader in veterinary education, Dr. Johnston has trained more than ten thousand vets in eleven countries on five continents and has written hundreds of articles for medical journals. She also conducts research at the University of Minnesota, specializing in small animal reproduction.

DR. MITCHELL BUSH

Dr. Bush, a University of California, Davis, graduate, cofounded New Opportunities in Animal Health Sciences (NOAHS) in 1991. As a result, he directs one of the most active vet training programs in the United States.

DR. TILAHUN D. YILMA

Dr. Yilma studies how tropical diseases are spread by animals. He directs a molecular biology research laboratory at the University of California, Davis. One of the world's leading public health veterinarians, he researches health problems that affect large groups of people.

DR. MURRAY FOWLER

Dr. Fowler founded the Zoological Medicine program at the University of California, Davis, the first of its kind in the world. The program trains vets to care for captive and privately owned wild animals.

You Can Be a Veterinarian!

Now that you have read this book, you know a lot more about what it's like to be a vet. You've met small animal veterinarians and wildlife specialists who explore the rainforest. You've seen veterinary technicians, groomers, and zookeepers at work. You've read about a vet who was launched into space!

Are you still interested in a career in veterinary medicine? Scott Yoder, the 4-H Club member showing off his fifteen-hundred-pound steer at the Ohio State Fair, hopes there's vet school in his future.

These are some of the qualities that the American Veterinary Medical Association thinks a vet should have:

- an inquiring mind

- keen powers of observation

- an interest in the biological sciences

- an appreciation for and understanding of animals

Does this describe you? Then go for it! It's never too early to start preparing. Turn the page to read about other sources you can contact to find out more about veterinary medicine.

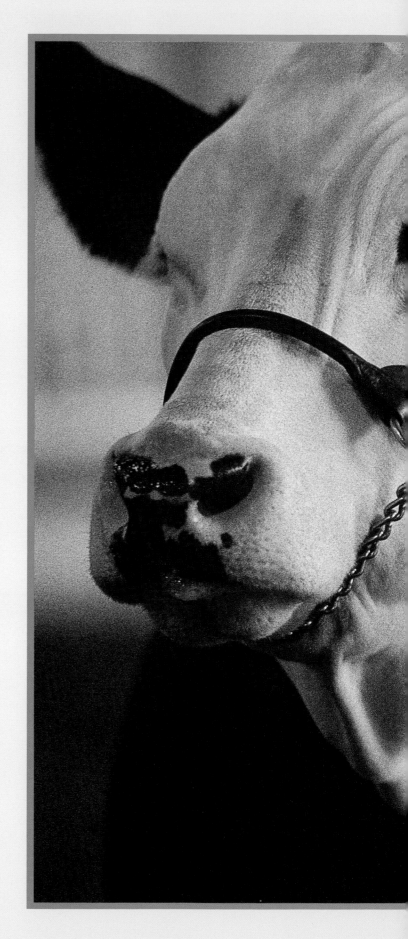

Other Sources of Information

GENERAL INFORMATION ABOUT VETERINARY CAREERS:

For information about the careers of veterinarian and veterinary technician, write for the free brochures "Today's Veterinarian" and "Your Career in Veterinary Technology." Send a large self-addressed, stamped envelope along with your written request to:

The American Veterinary Medical Association
1931 North Meacham Road
Suite 100
Schaumburg, IL 60173-4360

CONSERVATION:

National Wildlife Federation
Educational Materials
1400 16th Street NW
Washington, DC 20036

Request free information about careers in animal conservation.

World Wildlife Fund, Inc.
Public Information Office
1250 24th Street NW
Washington, DC 20037

Ask for free material about international wildlife conservation programs and careers.

The Wildlife Society
5410 Grosvenor Lane
Bethesda, MD 20814

Send fifty cents for the publication "A Wildlife Conservation Career for You."

THE HUMANE SOCIETY OF THE UNITED STATES:

Companion Animals Department
2100 L Street NW
Washington, DC 20037

For information about the society's programs, kids' clubs, and how to subscribe to the children's newsletter "Kind News," write to the Youth Education Division of the Humane Society:

National Association for Humane and Environmental Education
P.O. Box 362
East Hadam, CT 06423

American Animal Hospital Association
P.O. Box 150899
Denver, CO 80215-0899

ZOO PROGRAMS:
Many zoos have educational programs and/or internships for young people. These include:

Bronx Zoo
Wildlife Conservation Society
Education Department
2300 Southern Boulevard
Bronx, NY 10460-1199

Has a four-week summer internship program for teens. Teens receive intensive training and hands-on experience in working with keepers.

Cincinnati Zoo and Botanical Gardens "Zoo Academy" Program
Cincinnati Public Schools
Dr. Shelley J. Hamler
Career Path
P.O. Box 5381
Cincinnati, OH 45201-5381

A four-year special study program for grades 9–12. Students interested in working with animals can spend part of each school day at the zoo. They receive training in animal behavior and care and work directly with keepers and staff.

Audubon Institute
P.O. Box 4327
New Orleans, LA 70178

Junior zookeeping program for 7th and 8th graders. Volunteers in this program work throughout the school year to help with zookeeping chores and public education programs.

National Zoological Park
F.O.N.Z.
(Friends of the National Zoo)
Dept. of Education and Volunteer Services
3001 Connecticut Avenue NW
Washington, DC 20008

Ages 13–15. Summer programs involve learning about animal conservation and observing zoo professionals at work.

MARINE PARKS AND AQUARIUMS:

Sea World
Education Department
7007 Sea World Drive
Orlando, FL 32821

Summer programs for preschool (age 3) through grade 12 teach about marine animals and how staff works with them.

Sea World of California
Education Department
1720 South Shores Road
San Diego, CA 92109

Summer education classes for grades 10–12. Individual students must apply for admission.

National Aquarium
Pier 3, 501 East Pratt Street
Baltimore, MD 21202

Summer programs for grades 4–6.

4-H CLUB ACTIVITIES:

National 4-H Council
7100 Connecticut Avenue
Chevy Chase, MD 20815-4999

Request in writing information about national 4-H programs involving animal care, showing animals at fairs, and 4-H projects in veterinary science. Also, each state and county has its own 4-H programs. Consult headquarters in state capital for specific programs and events.

OTHER INTERNSHIPS:
Consult your local directory for specific internship programs being offered in private animal clinics and hospitals.

PHOTO CREDITS